DIVERSITY IN ACTION

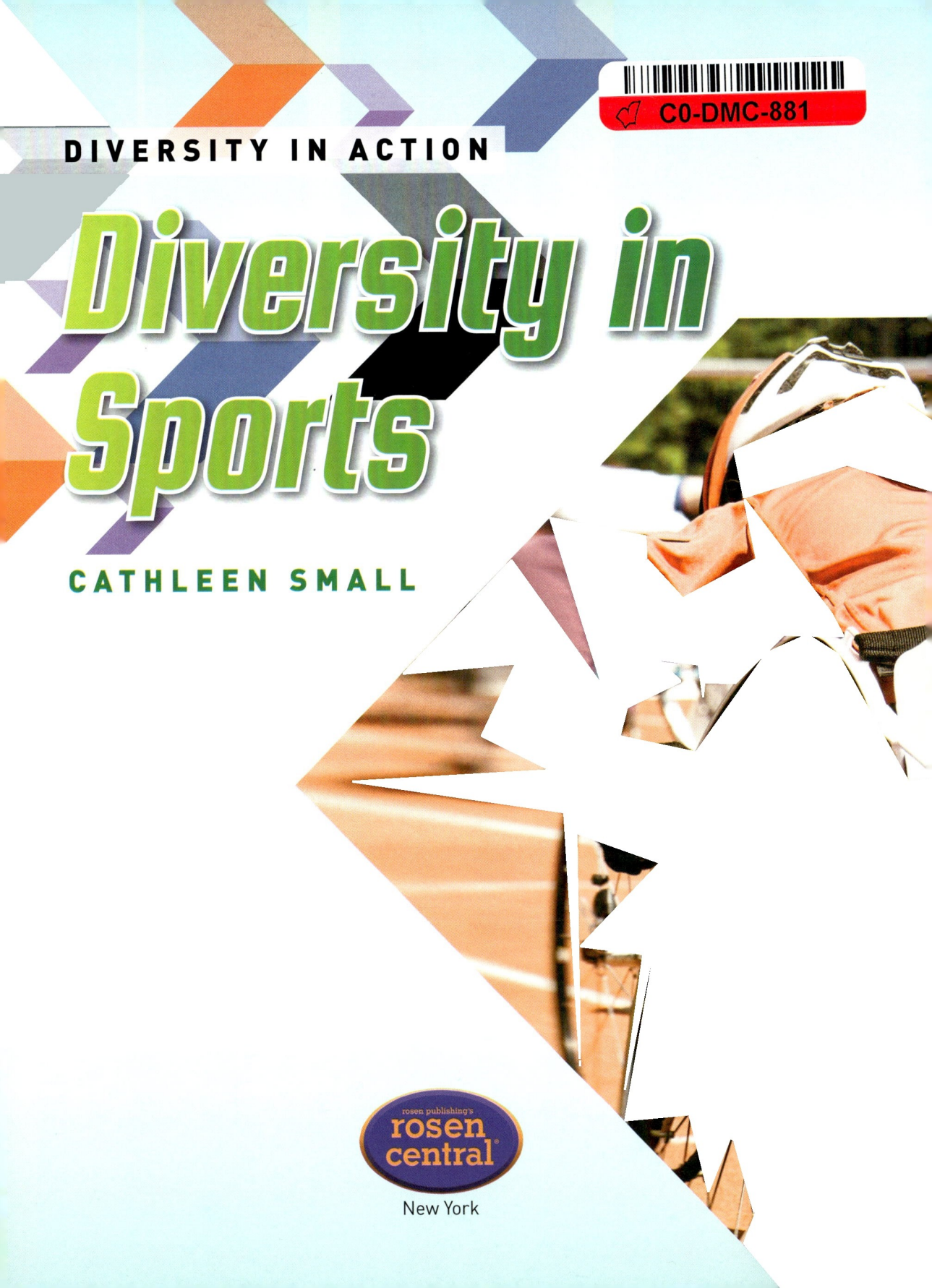

Diversity in Sports

CATHLEEN SMALL

rosen publishing's
rosen central®
New York

Published in 2019 by The Rosen Publishing Group, Inc.
29 East 21st Street
New York, NY 10010

Copyright © 2019 by The Rosen Publishing Group, Inc.

First Edition

All rights reserved. No part of this book may be reproduced in any form without permission in writing from the publisher, except by a reviewer.

Produced for Rosen by Calcium
Editors for Calcium: Sarah Eason and Jennifer Sanderson
Designer: Simon Borrough
Picture researcher: Rachel Blount

Photo credits: Cover photo of Mookie Betts: Wikimedia Commons/Arturo Pardavila III; Inside: Shutterstock: Jai Agnish: p. 22; Air Images: p. 24; Jefferson Bernardes: p. 31; Jose Luis Carrascosa: p. 36; CHEN WS: p. 41; Neale Cousland: p. 30; Everett Collection: p. 16; Keeton Gale: p. 17; Kathy Hutchins: p. 26; Jacob Lund: pp. 42–43; Gino Santa Maria: p. 28; Brian McEntire: p. 18; MediaPictures.pl: p. 37; Mezzotint: pp. 1, 5, 35; Monkey Business Images: p. 6; Photo Works: p. 23; Alessia Pierdomenico: p. 29; Pio3: p. 25; Juri Pozzi: p. 4; A.RICARDO: pp. 27, 34; Sirtravelalot: p. 7; Supannee Hickman: p. 39; Todd Taulman Photography: p. 11; Jamie Lamor Thompson: p. 19; Tinseltown: p. 8; Ververidis Vasilis: pp. 12–13b; Wavebreakmedia: p. 12; © UNHCR: Anthony Karumb: pp. 3, 33; Benjamin Loyseau: p. 32; Wikimedia Commons: Keith Allison: p. 8; Heath Campanaro: p. 38; Fernando Frazão/Agência Brasil: p. 40; Jay: p. 21; Arturo Pardavila III from Hoboken, NJ, USA: p. 10; Pathe Industries: p. 15; Noah Salzman: p. 20; Bob Sandberg: p. 14.

Cataloging-in-Publication Data

Names: Small, Cathleen.
Title: Diversity in sports / Cathleen Small.
Description: New York : Rosen Central, 2019. | Series: Diversity in action | Includes glossary and index.
Identifiers: ISBN 9781499440799 (pbk.) | ISBN 9781499440805 (library bound)
Subjects: LCSH: Sports—Juvenile literature. | Athletes—Juvenile literature. | Cultural pluralism—Juvenile literature. | Multiculturalism—Juvenile literature.
Classification: LCC GV705.4 S63 2019 | DDC 796—dc23

Manufactured in the United States of America

Contents

Chapter 1 Diversity on the Rise — 4

Chapter 2 Racial Diversity in Sports — 10

Chapter 3 Gender Diversity in Sports — 16

Chapter 4 Economic and Social Diversity in Sports — 22

Chapter 5 Cultural Diversity in Sports — 28

Chapter 6 Diverse Abilities in Sports — 34

Timeline — 44

Glossary — 46

For Further Reading — 47

Index — 48

Chapter 1
Diversity on the Rise

Sports—whether at amateur or professional level—is a field that lends itself well to diversity. At amateur levels, anyone who wants to play is usually welcome. At a professional level, people need a certain level of skill to make it onto a team. If they have the skills to do the sport, it should not really matter what their culture, ethnicity, or socioeconomic background is.

Sometimes, however, gender matters. For example, women are not recruited to play on professional baseball teams. However, they do play softball, so the opportunity to play still exists—the teams are just separated by gender. Ability matters in the same way that gender matters. There are very few people with disabilities who compete in sports at a professional level alongside nondisabled people. However, there are sporting leagues and organizations specifically for people with disabilities. For example, Special Olympics allows people with intellectual disabilities to compete in a large number of sporting events. The Paralympic Games allow athletes with a range of physical disabilities and impairments to participate in an event similar to the Olympic Games.

Sports are a great unifier: fans come in all genders, races, and abilities.

Diversity on the Rise

The Importance of Diversity in Sports

Diversity in sports has a number of benefits. It helps limit prejudice because athletes tend to respond to their teammates based on their ability in the sport, not based on factors such as culture, race, and socioeconomic background. Laura McAllister, Chairperson of Sport Wales, an organization that promotes athletics for all people in the country of Wales, commented, "It's all about championing the inclusivity of sport and showing that sport can be this really important lever for bringing people together, no matter what their…language or ability or belief."

Diversity in team sports is beneficial because it provides new ideas and unique skill sets. When team members are all very similar in their backgrounds, they sometimes become stuck in a particular way of thinking or playing, which makes it hard for the team to move forward. When people from diverse backgrounds are working together, it usually results in new and different ideas, one or more of which may be just what the team needs to take the lead. When people with different backgrounds are working together, team members have to concentrate harder to understand each other's strategies. The team members become more focused as they consider the strategies and plans brought up by their teammates.

Disability does not have to limit a person who wants to participate in sports.

Diversity in Sports

Encouraging diversity in sports has another benefit: It provides a much bigger pool of potential athletes to choose from. For example, if a football coach wanted to recruit only white male players who were at least six feet (1.8 m) tall, born into the middle class in the United States, and of a Christian faith, the pool of potential football players would be somewhat narrow. If the search was expanded to include anyone capable of playing the game well, regardless of size, social class, race, and cultural and religious background, there would be a much larger group of players to choose from.

Setting an Example

By encouraging diversity in sports, the sports field also sets a strong example for future generations. Children look up to athletes, and when they see a diverse group playing sports, it helps reinforce the idea that

Encouraging diversity and acceptance in sports at younger ages will help make diversity the norm in sports at the collegiate or professional level.

Diversity on the Rise

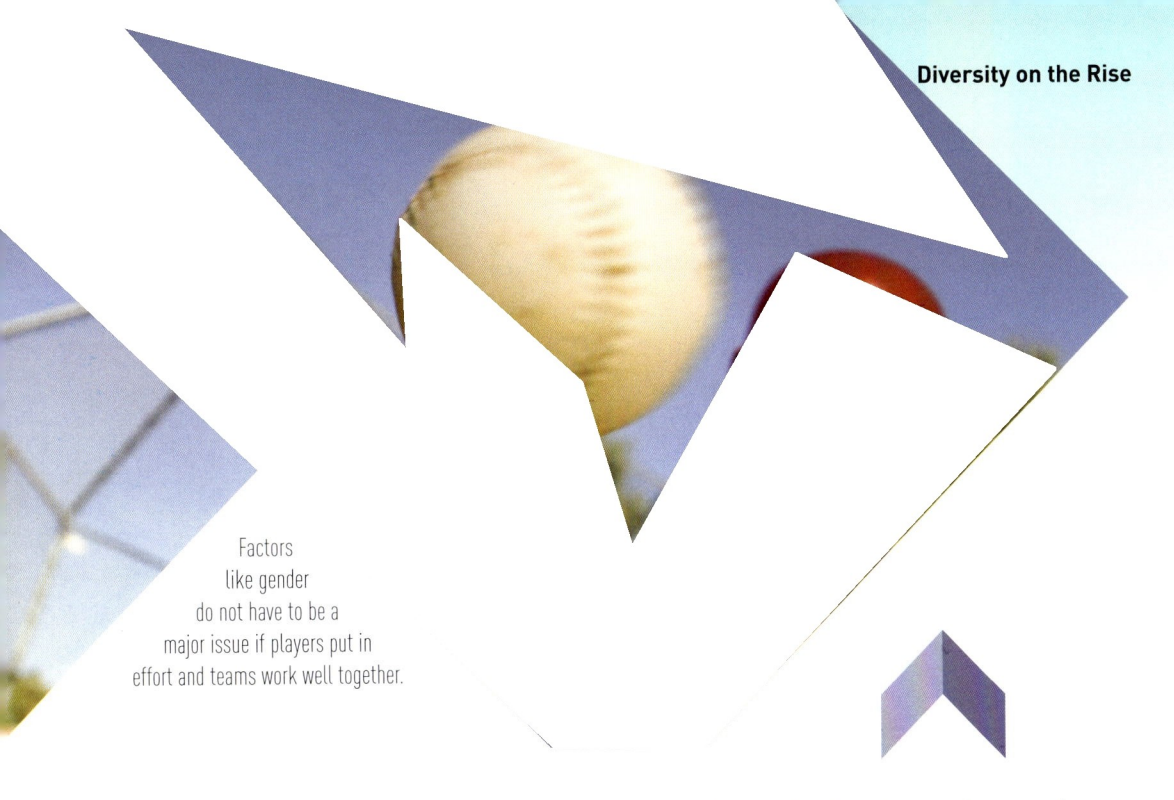

Factors like gender do not have to be a major issue if players put in effort and teams work well together.

anyone can play if he or she works hard. It also shows that on the playing field, ability and teamwork are what matter, not factors like a person's race or social status.

Richard Lapchick, director of the Institute for Diversity and Ethics in Sport (TIDES) at the University of Central Florida, says that race relations in communities are improved when the community has a diverse sports team. "When athletes are willing to speak out, people look up to them and listen to them," he says. So when the community sees diverse teams speaking out about issues like bullying and staying in school, the message is powerful.

Diversity in sports can also show the success that can come when many different people work together toward a common goal. Some sports are individual events, of course, but even in those, children can see the sportsmanship demonstrated between athletes. Sports also promote confidence in the athletes who participate in them. Not everyone is cut out to be the star quarterback, but everyone who contributes to the team can take pride in their game. That pride cultivates confidence in other areas of the person's life.

Diversity in Sports

Steph Curry:
NBA Superstar

Stephen (Steph) Curry is widely known as one of the greatest shooters in National Basketball Association (NBA) history. In the 2014–15 season, he led the Golden State Warriors to their first NBA championship in forty years and won the title of Most Valuable Player (MVP) in the NBA. The next year, he won the coveted award again, but this time he was also the first player ever to be unanimously voted MVP.

Recordbreaking Talent

In his years playing college and professional basketball, Curry has broken many records. It is perhaps not surprising, given that he comes from a basketball family. His father Dell was also an NBA player and his younger brother Seth also plays in the NBA. Dell Curry spent much of his NBA career with the Charlotte Hornets, and Steph and Seth would tag along to their father's games. The two boys would practice shooting with the Hornets during pregame warmups.

Curry is a bit different from a typical NBA star. He is not as tall as some of the other players at only 6 foot 3 inches (190 cm). He is also rather slim. Curry wanted to play college basketball for Virginia Tech, where his father had gone, but Virginia Tech did not recruit him because he was much thinner than most successful players. Curry ended up playing for Davidson College in North Carolina, which recognized the raw talent in young Curry.

Steph began dating his wife Ayesha when she was pursuing an acting career in Los Angeles and he was at college. They have two daughters.

Diversity on the Rise

It was a wise move by Davidson, as Curry proved his talent and won many awards during his time playing for the school.

Humble and Hard Working

Large egos are fairly common in the NBA, but Curry is known for being humble and an extremely hard worker. He is also a devout Christian and does not hide his faith.

Since 2011, Curry has been married to his college sweetheart, Ayesha, whom he first met at church camp. He is outspoken about his pride in her talent and ambition in her own career—she is a celebrity chef, cookbook author, and television personality. NBA stars are not typically known for maintaining successful marriages, which makes Steph and Ayesha Curry unique in their devotion to each other and their family.

CURRY'S AWARDS

At Davidson College, Curry is the all-time leading scorer. He is also a two-time NBA champion and has been NBA MVP twice. He has been on the NBA All-Star team five times, too. His list of achievements will continue to grow as long as he plays.

Chapter 2
Racial Diversity in Sports

While sports is a field that lends itself well to diversity, in reality there is a definite lack of certain types of diversity, especially in professional sports.

Markus Lynn Betts is a formidable and well-known MLB player.

Stereotypes

Certain stereotypes exist in the world of sports. Many people think most of the great basketball players are black. There is a perception that there is a fair number of black players in professional football, too. Figure skating is thought to be a sport for white women and men, while Major League Baseball (MLB) is thought to be played by white and Dominican men.

Sometimes, these stereotypes are true. In the NBA, 74 percent of the players are black. The vast majority of figure skaters are white, with Asian figure skaters coming second in numbers on US teams. Black figure skaters are few and far between. MLB does have mostly white players (60 percent), with Dominican and other Latinx players coming in second at 30 percent. There are, however, exceptions to the rule. Right fielder for the Boston Red Sox Mookie (Markus Lynn) Betts is black.

One Diverse League

Research suggests that only one professional sports league in the United States is truly racially diverse, where one particular ethnicity does not make up at least 50 percent of the players. That is Major League Soccer (MLS).

Racial Diversity in Sports

In MLS, close to 48 percent of players are white, 25 percent are Latinx, 10 percent are black, and almost 20 percent are considered another nonwhite race. The only race that is decidedly absent in MLS is Asian; there are very few Asian players.

In professional sports, something called Simpson's Diversity Index can be used to determine diversity. This index uses mathematical formulas to determine how likely it is that two players selected at random in a league will be the same race. In MLS Simpson's Diversity Index indicates that there is only a 32 percent chance that two players chosen at random will be the same race. As a comparison, in the NBA the Simpson's Diversity Index shows that there is a 66 percent that both players chosen at random will be the same race—and a 58 percent chance that both will be black.

The National Football League (NFL) is also dominated by black players, with 65 percent belonging to that ethnicity.

11

Diversity in Sports

Diversity Benefits Soccer

MLS provides a great example of why diversity is beneficial in sports. A 2014 study published in the *Washington Post* looked at how diversity on the soccer field benefited soccer teams.

One thing the researchers noted was that in soccer, all team members are involved in the same pursuit: scoring goals and winning the game. That is the case in most sports, and the importance of it is that a common goal allows the talents and insights that each team member brings to be highlighted. When players are working toward different goals, it can sometimes be difficult to see how much benefit diverse backgrounds bring. When everyone is engaged in a common goal, it is easy to see how different approaches benefit the whole team.

Players with different backgrounds interpret problems on the field or on the court differently because they have been exposed to different methods of training and styles of play. They use their skills in different ways to solve problems, which makes it decidedly more difficult for the opposing team to mount a defense.

Football in Europe

Soccer teams in the United States are quite ethnically diverse, with players coming from not only the United States but other countries, too. However, teams playing in Europe are even more ethnically diverse. Soccer (called football in Europe) is an incredibly popular sport in Europe, and European teams recruit players from nearly fifty different nationalities.

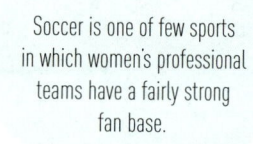

Soccer is one of few sports in which women's professional teams have a fairly strong fan base.

Racial Diversity in Sports

CRITICAL THINKING QUESTION: How do you think the United States and other countries could begin to encourage greater diversity in their sports teams?

The researchers behind the 2014 study published in the *Washington Post* used a mathematical formula involving goals scored, goals conceded, and each player's market value (what the player would cost to buy or sell from or to another club) to determine how a team's diversity affects its performance. The results were clear: The more ethnically diverse a team was, the stronger its performance on the field. The researchers did a second study using a different mathematical model and found exactly the same results.

The researchers also suggested another benefit to racial diversity on the soccer field: Less diverse teams can benefit from playing against diverse teams because they are exposed to the different playing styles and techniques used by the more diverse teams, and can incorporate those into their own play.

Like other European soccer clubs, Manchester United has a diverse team of players.

Diversity in Sports

Jackie Robinson:
Black Baseball Hero

In the 1880s, black and Latinx men played baseball in professional leagues known as the Negro leagues. The Negro leagues existed until they began to decline in the late 1940s. In 1958, when the civil rights movement was in its early days, the last Negro league folded.

Making History

Just as the Negro leagues were beginning to fold, a young man named Jackie Robinson made history. On April 15, 1947, he broke the color barrier and became the first black man to play MLB. That same year, Robinson was named MLB's Rookie of the Year and in 1949, he became the first black player to win the National League's MVP award.

A Rough Start to a Glorious Career

Robinson's start with the Dodgers was rough. Many players were not happy to see him join the team, and suggested that they would rather sit out than play on the team with Robinson. The team manager took a hard line, though, defending Robinson's talent and his right to play.

Baseball great Jackie Robinson was born to sharecropper parents and was the youngest of five children.

Racial Diversity in Sports

He suggested that those who did not want to play with Robinson could leave the team. Some teams threatened to stage a walkout in games against the Dodgers and to spread the walkout across the entire league. The president and baseball commissioner of the National League spoke out. He announced that players who engaged in a strike would be suspended.

Robinson not only broke the color barrier, he also achieved a lot of other accolades. He was the first professional athlete in any sport to have his uniform number (42) retired across all teams in the league. April 15 is now designated as Jackie Robinson Day in MLB, and all players on every team wear Robinson's number on that day.

Life After Baseball

After his retirement, Robinson became the first black television analyst in MLB and expanded his interests to become the first black vice president of a major US corporation. Robinson was also well known for his contributions to the civil rights movement and his belief in nonviolence. It was an interesting switch, since Robinson had, in his younger days, joined a Southern California gang. Robinson grew up poor in a rich area of Los Angeles and he was definitely out of place among his much wealthier classmates.

Jackie Robinson died in 1972 at just fifty-three years old. He was posthumously awarded the Presidential Medal of Freedom and the Congressional Gold Medal.

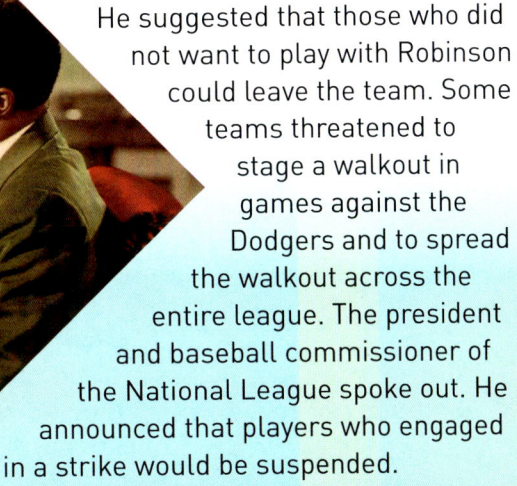

THE JACKIE ROBINSON STORY
So notable were Robinson's contributions to baseball that a 1950 movie was made about his entry into MLB. Robinson played himself as an adult, but the film begins when he is just a child. It traces his journey as a talented college athlete to his playing in the Negro leagues. Robinson's rise into MLB is chronicled as he is scouted by the Brooklyn Dodgers. While playing with the Dodgers, he faces bigotry from fans and teammates but pushes his way through a playing slump to eventually prove his worth as a player.

Chapter 3
Gender Diversity in Sports

Gender diversity is an interesting topic in sports because it exists, but it also does not exist. Many sports are segregated into male and female teams, so while both genders have the opportunity to play, they do not play together. Often, the male teams get far more attention than the female teams. For example, both men and women can play professional basketball, but they do not play together. Professional male players join the NBA, and professional female players play in the Women's NBA, or WNBA. Baseball players have MLB, which does not include women. Female players instead play softball in the National Pro Fastpitch (NPF).

A Women's League

From 1943 to 1954, female baseball players participated in the All-American Girls Professional Baseball League. The league was started when men were

Women had a chance to play baseball when male players were away fighting in World War II.

Gender Diversity in Sports

CRITICAL THINKING QUESTION: What do you think makes male professional sports so much more popular than female professional sports?

away fighting in World War II, because baseball executives wanted to keep America's Pastime, as baseball has been called, in the public eye. The popularity of the league diminished after the war, but it was the subject of a popular 1992 film called *A League of Their Own*.

Why the Popularity Difference?

In professional sports, male leagues are almost always much more popular than female leagues among viewers. The author of an article on whether professional sports could ever have men and women in the same leagues wrote in the *New York Times* that professional female sports are simply not moneymakers. Their athletes are compensated far differently because of it, too. For example, in 2014, forward Kevin Garnett of the Boston Celtics earned $21 million per year plus endorsements. In contrast, the WNBA's Tamika Catchings of the Indiana Fever earned $4 million for her entire career, including endorsements. Per year, she earned the league maximum of $105,000. That is different from Kevin Garnett's $21 million per year—and it is $300,000 per year less than the NBA league minimum.

Although Tamika Catchings was one of WNBA's greatest, she earned considerably less than her male counterparts.

Integrate—or Not?

There has been some talk about integrating professional sports in order to promote gender equality. A few years ago, Mark Cuban, the owner of the Dallas Mavericks, considered drafting Brittney Griner to his NBA team after she led her Baylor University basketball team to an undefeated season. And MLB has considered recruiting female players in the past who have performed exceptionally well on their high school or college teams.

Diversity in Sports

Problems with Integration

People who oppose the idea of integrating leagues point out a several problems. First, men, as a general rule, are larger and stronger than women. It is not discrimination; it is physiology. So, there is a fear that women competing alongside men could be injured, particularly in some of the more physically demanding contact sports.

There is also a thought that men might compete differently if they are competing in these sports along with women. They might go easier on their female counterparts, for fear of accidentally hurting them. And there is concern that men would be more aggressive to females playing alongside them, if they were frustrated with their sport being opened to women.

There is also concern that it would be frustrating for women to be incorporated into men's professional sports because their best play may not be as good as their male counterparts, because, again, male players tend to be larger and stronger. Stars like Tamika Catchings can shine in the WNBA, but they would undoubtedly be outshone by some of the male stars of the NBA.

Coed teams are becoming more and more commonplace in sports at young ages.

The thought behind coed professional sports teams is that the change would have to start earlier, in high school and college sports, for example. At the elementary school level, sports are sometimes coed and sometimes not. To promote gender inclusion at a professional level in sports, integration would first have to take place at the lower levels.

Gender Diversity in Sports

Benefits to Coed Sports

Certainly, there are benefits to coed sports. When done right, coed teams can result in players that recognize each other's skills, rather than their gender differences. They can also promote mutual respect between the genders, as players recognize the strengths that players of the opposite gender bring to the team. Team sports also necessarily promote cooperation. Players have to cooperate and work together to win. Team sports promote confidence. When players perform well, it increases their confidence. On a coed team, when players perform well against both male and female peers, it further increases their confidence. A female who performs well on a coed basketball team is not just good "for a woman"—she is just plain good. Whether professional sports will ever go coed remains to be seen, but certainly there are benefits to considering the possibility.

CRITICAL THINKING QUESTION:
Which sports do you think best lend themselves to being coed, and why?

Most group sports are played by same-sex teams. Some people argue that female players would be better challenged if these sports became coed.

Diversity in Sports

Abby Wambach:
Six-Time US Soccer Athlete of the Year

Many of the most recognizable names in major sports are men—which is unsurprising, given that men's leagues dominate most of the sports that are broadcast on television. When women's names are known for sports, it tends to be in sports traditionally associated with women, such as figure skating, or individual sports, like skiing. But then, there is Abby Wambach.

Taking Notice of Women

Soccer is one of the few team sports that has a fairly significant female presence in the United States. Perhaps it is because soccer is one of the country's newer sports and has only really gained popularity in the United States in the last few decades. When other sports such as basketball and baseball started gaining popularity, women were not really a part of competitive sports. However, by the time soccer came around, it was not unusual for women to be involved in sports.

Abby Wambach is the world record holder across genders for international goals scored.

People in the United States really took notice of women's soccer when the women's national soccer team won three World Cups and four Olympic gold medals. Since the early 1990s, women's soccer has had several standout players, including Mia Hamm, Hope Solo, and Brandi Chastain. Abby Wambach is a standout even among them. She holds the record as the highest goal-scorer of all time for the US women's national team and the world record for international goals scored among both male and female soccer players. She was named FIFA's World Player of the Year in 2012, beating out exceptional male players to become the first woman to hold that title in a decade.

Wambach Is a Winner

Wambach has played in four FIFA Women's World Cups from 2003 to 2015 (the competition is held every four years) and was a champion in the 2011 and 2015 competitions. She also played in the 2004 and 2012 Summer Olympics, winning gold medals in both. She has been named US Soccer Athlete of the Year six times.

Wambach credits growing up as the youngest of seven children in her family for her competitive drive and ability to play on a team. From her six older siblings, she learned competition but also humility—both characteristics that make her an extremely strong athlete.

WOMEN IN US SOCCER
The US Women's National Soccer Team (USWNT) is the most successful team in international women's soccer. The team won the first Women's World Cup title (in 1991) and has won two more World Cup titles since. It has also won Olympic gold four times. The USWNT won medals in every Olympics and every World Cup from 1991 to 2015. In the FIFA Women's World Rankings, the team was first from 2008 to 2014.

Chapter 4
Economic and Social Diversity in Sports

Although players are judged on their ability, not on characteristics such as race, cultural background, and economic background, socioeconomic factors do come into play in sports.

Socioeconomics and Sports

Some sports are dominated by athletes from wealthy backgrounds. For example, the National Hockey League (NHL) is made up of 93 percent white players. Researchers speculate that this is because hockey is an expensive sport to play.

Thomas Wilson, a sociologist from Florida Atlantic University, conducted a study that showed that the wealthier people were, the more likely they were to participate in sports. He stated that those from wealthy backgrounds were more involved in sports because they could better afford them both financially and in terms of having leisure time.

Hockey is a very expensive sport to play. Players need a lot of equipment but they also need access to a rink.

Soccer is an accessible sport to play even for people from lower socioeconomic backgrounds. All you really need is a field, a ball, and a couple of goals.

CRITICAL THINKING QUESTION: According to a Nielsen study, the NHL has the richest audience of any sport in the United States, with one-third of viewers making more than $100,000 per year. MLS has the poorest, with nearly half of its viewers making less than $40,000 per year. Why do you think this is? Where do you think other sports fall in viewer financial worth, and why?

People from poor or working-class backgrounds often work multiple jobs or overtime, and they often do not have the money, time, or energy left to participate in sports.

Wilson also found that when wealthier people are interested in or participate in a sport, they tend to share that enjoyment with their friends, who are likely also from wealthier backgrounds. The sport then becomes dominated by fans and players from a certain economic background. Increasing economic diversity in sports would increase the diversity in viewership, which would result in an even more level playing field in the world of sports.

A Drop in Participation

Recent studies also show that sports participation is dropping in lower-income communities, while it stays strong in higher-income communities. In a 2015 study in Massachusetts, researchers found that in the state's ten poorest communities, participation in sports was 43 percent below the state average. The same study showed that in the ten wealthiest communities, participation in sports was 32 percent above the statewide average.

The problem with this lack of economic diversity in sports is that it limits the possible success of students and young adults. According to Robert Putnam, a political science professor at Harvard University, extracurricular activities like sports teach participants how to have good work habits, self-discipline, leadership qualities, a sense of teamwork, and a sense of civic engagement.

Diversity in Sports

Students who participate in sports often achieve better grades in school, and have better study habits and a lower dropout rate. These skills translate to strong college skills and better preparation for the workforce.

Budget Cuts

In addition to simply not being able to afford to participate, some students face challenges with becoming involved in sports, because the schools they go to have cut funding for sports as a way to make up for deficits in their budget. If the school cannot afford to host the sport, chances are that the students will be unable to find a way to play on a formal team.

For sports programs outside schools, there are financial problems, too. Wealthy communities tend to donate time and money to programs that encourage youth participation in sports. Poor communities cannot afford to do that, so children in these communities have far fewer opportunities to participate in sports. If a student cannot join a baseball team, either at school or as part of a community program, then he or she will not learn to play the sport or improve his or her skills. It is unlikely that he or she will ever be a professional in that sport.

There are, however, a few rags-to-riches stories of talented children from poor backgrounds who have been able to play sports (sometimes thanks to scholarships) and have made a successful career out of it. However, studies have shown that children from poorer backgrounds are less likely to make it to the professional level.

Wealthier schools often have coveted sports programs.

Economic and Social Diversity in Sports

CRITICAL THINKING QUESTION:
What ways can you think of to encourage more economic diversity among athletes?

Pickup games of basketball are popular in all kinds of neighborhoods.

Sports for the Working Class

Two sports that do tend to be available to students in poorer areas are football and basketball. These are popular sports in the United States, so many schools—even the poorer ones—offer them as possible activities. Basketball is easy to play in terms of finding an open court at a park or school. Even in less fortunate communities, children can often find an open basketball court, grab a ball and some friends, and practice their skills. However, that is a little harder to do with sports that require a larger or more complicated field or rink.

25

Diversity in Sports

LeBron James:
From Poverty to NBA Success

Some athletes, such as Steph Curry, grow up in comfortable or even privileged homes. They attend schools with good programs, where they can play sports. Then there are athletes who grow up in poor or unfortunate circumstances and, despite the challenges of that upbringing, manage to excel and come out at the top.

A Tough Life

LeBron James is one of these success stories. Like Steph Curry, he is a talented athlete, but his early life and introduction to sports could not have been more different than Curry's.

James was born to a sixteen-year-old single mother, Gloria Marie James. Gloria was unable to find steady work, so she and LeBron moved frequently, living in apartments in the poor parts of Akron, Ohio. Gloria wanted her son to have more stability in his life, so when he was in elementary school, she allowed him to live with a local youth football coach, Frank Walker. Walker first introduced James to basketball when he was nine years old.

A Shooting Star

James was part of the Northeast Ohio Shooting Stars, a youth basketball team. Along with his three close friends, he took the team to local and national success. The

GIVING BACK

LeBron James may be a megastar, but he also gives back, especially to Akron, Ohio. James started the LeBron James Family Foundation, which mostly focuses on education and the children of Akron. He hopes that children reached by the foundation will recognize their gifts and pursue their education to make the best use of those gifts.

Economic and Social Diversity in Sports

boys' skills gained local recognition, and they were able to attend a private Catholic high school made up of mostly white, wealthier students.

James started on the team at St. Vincent–St. Mary High School as a freshman, averaging twenty-one points per game. He helped take the team to an undefeated season and a Division III state title. After James' sophomore year, a writer for *SLAM* magazine called him possibly the best high school basketball player in the United States. During high school, James became the first high school basketball underclassman to appear on the cover of *Sports Illustrated*, a highly popular sports publication.

In high school, James was equally talented in football. He was recruited by top colleges, but he opted to pursue basketball instead. He also chose to forego college, going straight from high school to the NBA instead. While that would be a risky move for many, James had enough raw talent to know that his chances of success as a professional player were very good.

James shows his skill as he dunks the ball as number 23 for the Cavaliers.

Chapter 5
Cultural Diversity in Sports

Race and culture are not the same thing. Race refers to divisions of people based on certain physical characteristics, such as the color of their skin. Culture, however refers to the customs, social norms, achievements, and arts of a particular group of people.

Sometimes culture is tied to a particular race, but not always. For example, not all black people belong to the same cultural group. Black people who came to the United States from Africa have different cultural norms and customs from those whose families have been in the United States for generations. Native Americans all belong to one racial group, but they have many different cultural groups based on their specific tribes.

Sometimes cultures are referred to in umbrella terms, such as when someone refers to "Native American culture." There probably are some customs and norms that are common to most Native Americans, regardless of tribe. However, digging down a little deeper shows that even within a particular race, there are different cultural groups.

Sometimes culture and race are intertwined, but sometimes they differ.

Cultural Diversity in Sports

A Cultural Melting Pot

The United States is made up of many different cultural groups because it is a nation of immigrants. The land was originally inhabited by Native Americans, and then white Europeans, British, and Scandinavians immigrated and settled. Slaves were brought over from Africa, and people from Mexico and Central America immigrated, too. The United States still welcomes many immigrants every year. For all of these cultures to live together in harmony, it is important for people to respect other cultures. Showcasing cultural diversity in sports is one way to do that.

Sports, the Great Equalizer

Former South African President Nelson Mandela, whose country was long divided by opposing races and cultures, once said, "Sport has the power to change the world. It has the power to inspire. It has the power to unite people in a way that little else does. Sport can awaken hope where there was previously only despair. Sport speaks to people in a language they can understand."

The United Nations (UN) states, "Sport has been increasingly recognized and used as a low-cost and high-impact tool in humanitarian, development and peace-building efforts."

The late Nelson Mandela believed in the unifying power of sports. He was passionate about giving all children the chance to play sports.

CRITICAL THINKING QUESTION:
What other pastimes have a similar uniting power to that of sports? How do they unite people of different cultures?

29

Diversity in Sports

On the playing field, on the court, or on the ice, players relate to one another based on sport. They do not focus on culture; they focus on the game, on teamwork, and on a common goal of winning. On the field, they are united, even if they might be less connected off the field.

Australia is an extremely diverse country, with native cultures, lifelong Australians, and many immigrants. The Australian Football League (AFL) has recently been making a strong effort to promote cultural diversity in sports in an effort to promote general social inclusion. Current AFL teams are composed of 11 percent indigenous players and 14 percent multicultural players.

Youth Sports and Culture

In youth sports, cultural diversity is extremely beneficial. Students from different cultural backgrounds can, as part of a sports team, establish friendships, feel as if they are a contributing part of a community, and, if the language used in the sport is not their first language, gain practice in that language.

CRITICAL THINKING QUESTION: What do you think can be done in the United States and other countries to encourage cultural diversity in sports?

AFL players are mostly white, but the league is working to attract players of different cultures to improve its diversity.

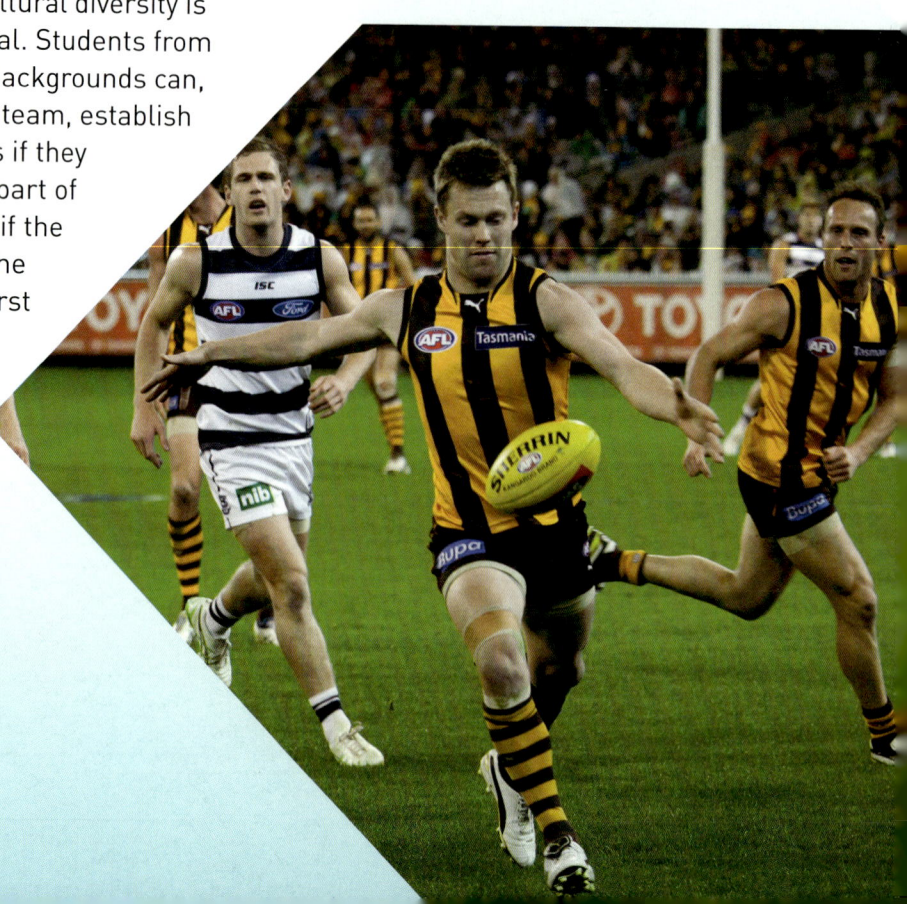

Cultural Diversity in Sports

Opening ceremonies are typically amazing displays of different cultures.

Benefits of Cultural Diversity in Sports

Cultural diversity in sports is a learning experience for the audience, too. In major worldwide events, such as the Olympic Games or World Cup soccer, ceremonies surrounding the games tend to highlight the unique customs and cultural elements of people from different countries. It is a great way for spectators to learn more about other countries' cultures.

Cultural diversity in sports is also good from a competitive aspect. People from different cultures bring different strategies, viewpoints, and problem-solving methods to the game. Teammates from different cultures can work together to devise strategies for the team that they might not otherwise think of if all the players came from the same background. Players also learn a lot from diverse opponents. When a diverse team plays, it may use new strategies and plays that the other team may not have seen before. The other team can then incorporate that into its own play.

Encouraging cultural diversity in sports opens up the pool of potential athletes to choose from. If a team recruits from only one cultural group, it may not have many athletes to choose from. If it expands its net to include all cultural groups, the number of athletes to choose from increases substantially.

Diversity in Sports

The Refugee Olympic Team:
Giving Refugees Hope

Athletes come to the Olympic Games from many countries and all different cultures. However, there is one team that embraces a number of cultures: the Refugee Olympic Team (ROT).

Normally at the Olympic Games, athletes represent the country of their citizenship. However, in 2016, the International Olympic Committee (IOC) decided that to show solidarity with the world's refugees, they would allow some refugees to compete at the Summer Olympics as one team.

Heartwarming Stories

The athletes competed in several track and field events, swimming, and judo, and their stories are both heartbreaking and heartwarming.

Yusra Mardini is a Syrian refugee who fled from Turkey to Greece in an inflatable boat. Partway through the journey, the boat started to take on water, forcing her to swim. Thankfully, Mardini is a strong swimmer—she later swam in the 2016 100m freestyle.

CHANGING JUSTICE

Even people who may not watch much of the Olympic Games often tune in to see the opening and closing ceremonies. The ceremonies are impressive displays of color, light, sound, and dramatic effects. They also make for an impressive showcase of different cultures and talents.

Cultural Diversity in Sports

Yolande Mabika is originally from the Democratic Republic of Congo. She was separated from her parents as a result of the Second Congo War and lived in a children's home. She started practicing judo and traveled to Brazil for a competition. While there, her coaches left her and her fellow judoka Popole Misenga confined in their hotel room with very little food. Mabika escaped and wandered the streets for two days before finding help. Mabika and Misenga went on to become part of the judo ROT.

Five of the athletes in the ROT were originally from war-torn South Sudan and fled to safety in Kenya. Anjelina Lohalith was only eight when she left for Kenya, and she later went on to complete in the 2016 500m race. Rose Lokonyen participated in the 800m race. Yiech Biel ran in the 800m. James Chiengjiek left South Sudan when he was thirteen to avoid being recruited as a child soldier. He competed in the 2016 400m. Athlete Paulo Lokoro ran in the 1500m.

Rami Anis was a swimmer even before his home country of Syria became ravaged by war. When his hometown of Aleppo suffered massive destruction in the Syrian Civil War, Anis fled to Belgium by way of Turkey and Greece, having to travel between the latter two by inflatable dinghy. He swam in the 2016 Olympic Games 100m butterfly.

Like Anis, Yonas Kinde from Ethiopia was an athlete long before he became a refugee. However, he was unable to compete in the Olympics because of his refugee status—until the ROT formed.

Refugee athletes including ROT members from the Tegla Loroupe Refugee Athletes Training Center regularly take part in a morning run within Ngong's township.

Chapter 6
Diverse Abilities in Sports

Much like gender diversity, diverse abilities in sports are both welcomed and segregated. Nearly every sport you can think of is available to people with all abilities but very often, people with disabilities participate in disability-specific competitions rather than alongside nondisabled athletes.

Why Segregate?

Segregating disabled and nondisabled athletes levels the playing field. Often disabled athletes are just not going to compete at the same level as nondisabled athletes, and few people want to compete in a sport where they have no chance of winning. After all, sports are meant to be about fun and teamwork, but most athletes would also like the chance to win. So segregating sports into disabled and nondisabled categories ensures that people of all abilities are able to compete against people with similar abilities.

Wheelchair basketball is popular among men and women in wheelchairs.

Why Include?

That being said, segregating athletes does not do much for social inclusion. Today, there is a large movement to try to promote inclusion and integrate all different types of people in the general community. One way to show that people with disabilities are "more alike than different"—a popular saying in the disability community—is to have disabled athletes compete alongside nondisabled athletes.

34

For those with mobility challenges, many road races, particularly city marathons, have a category especially for wheelchair users.

Disabled Athletes Who Participate in Nondisabled Competitions

There are some athletes with disabilities who have competed at very high levels against nondisabled athletes. For example, in 1904, George Eyser from America won multiple Olympic medals in gymnastics, despite having a wooden leg. Olivér Halassy was a Hungarian water polo player who competed in the Olympics three times and earned two gold medals and one silver, despite having a leg amputated as a child. Hungarian shooter Karoly Takacs competed in two Olympic games, despite having his right arm amputated after he was injured by a faulty grenade—he learned to shoot with his left hand. Lis Hartel from Denmark broke a number of barriers in the 1952 Olympics, where she competed in equestrian dressage. She was one of the first women allowed to compete against men in the event, and she was paralyzed below both knees as a result of polio. Hartel learned how to compensate for the unusable muscles. She won a silver medal in the Olympics.

CRITICAL THINKING QUESTION: Participation in sports starts at an early age for most people. What are some things you think schools can do to encourage students of all abilities to participate?

Diversity in Sports

Ildikó Újlaky-Rejtő, a Hungarian woman who competed in fencing in the Olympics, was born deaf and had to learn fencing based on written instructions, instead of by hearing them, as most athletes do. She earned two gold medals, one silver, and one bronze in the three Olympic Games she competed in. Im Dong Hyun, a South Korean archer who has only 10 percent vision in one eye and 20 percent in the other, led the South Korean team to a bronze medal in the 2012 Olympic Games and set the first world record of the Games that year.

In a heartwarming moment in 1984, US swimmer Jeff Float, who has only 20 percent hearing in one ear and 40 percent in the other, gained a huge lead for the United States during a relay swimming event in the 1984 Olympic Games. The crowd cheered so loudly that Float was able to hear them—the first time he had ever heard a crowd cheering him. Similarly, Terence Parkin of South Africa won the silver medal for breaststroke in the 2000 Olympic Games, even though the start of the race had to be signaled to him by strobe light, since he is completely deaf.

Swimming is a sport that many people with physical disabilities can participate in.

In 1984, Neroli Fairhall of New Zealand became the first person to compete in the Olympics after also competing in the Paralympics. Fairhall is paralyzed from the waist down and uses a wheelchair, yet she still competed in the women's archery.

Diverse Abilities in Sports

CRITICAL THINKING QUESTION: What are some of the specific benefits of athletes competing in inclusive competitions, rather than in events separated by ability?

Italian Paola Fantato, who is also an archer, reached a similar goal when she became the first person to compete in the Olympics and the Paralympics the same year.

Marla Runyan, an Olympic runner, is legally blind. She won five gold medals in the Paralympics and went on to compete in the Olympics. Natalie du Toit is a South African swimmer who lost her left leg below the knee but still qualified for the Olympics. Du Toit had barely missed qualifying for the 2000 Olympic team, and in 2001 was hit by a car and lost her lower leg. She competed in the 2004 Paralympics where she won five gold medals and one silver medal. Du Toit persevered and qualified for the 2008 Olympic Games.

Stories like these show the possibilities for highly skilled athletes who just happen to have a disability. But for those athletes with disabilities who are not at Olympic or world-class level but who still want to compete, there are the Paralympics and Special Olympics.

Athletic crutches allow this soccer player to participate in the game despite him having one amputated leg.

Diversity in Sports

Paralympics

The Paralympics began in 1948, featuring a small group of British World War II veterans. Now, thousands of athletes compete from more than 150 countries every Olympic year. The Paralympics is designed to be an Olympic-type competitive event for athletes with a wide range of physical disabilities and visual impairments. The event also accepts some athletes with intellectual disabilities, though more commonly those athletes compete in Special Olympics.

Special Olympics

In 1968, Eunice Kennedy Shriver, sister to President John F. Kennedy, started Special Olympics. Although few people knew it, when John F. Kennedy took office, the large Kennedy family included a member with intellectual disabilities: John and Eunice's sister, Rosemary. She was born with an intellectual disability that resulted in her having the mental capacity of a child of around twelve years old. Her father, Joseph, felt Rosemary's disability was such an embarrassment to the family that he took her for an experimental

The women's 100m butterfly medalists at the 2008 Paralympic Games were Annabelle Williams (bronze), Natalie du Toit (gold), and Ellie Cole (silver).

Diverse Abilities in Sports

treatment: a lobotomy. The treatment failed, and Rosemary was left with the mental capacity of a toddler and was confined to a mental institution for the rest of her life. The sad story of Rosemary Kennedy is part of what inspired Eunice to begin Special Olympics. She was working on President John F. Kennedy's panel to benefit people with intellectual disabilities, and she was well aware of the benefits of sports and physical activity to people with intellectual disabilities. Sports could help them build confidence and perform better at school and work. Combining that knowledge with her knowledge of her sister's fate, Eunice created Special Olympics.

Today the Special Olympics organization holds competitions in numerous sports in hundreds of countries around the world. More than 5.7 million athletes with intellectual disabilities participate in Special Olympics. Competitions happen at different times year-round, rather than being tied to the schedule of the Olympic Games. But every other year, much like the Olympic Games, the Special Olympics World Games takes place.

Special Olympics is widely enjoyed by people with developmental and intellectual disabilities who wish to participate in competitive sports.

Benefits of Diversity

Whether athletes compete in segregated groups, like they do for the Paralympics or Special Olympics, or they compete alongside nondisabled athletes, many of the benefits are the same. Athletes of all abilities gain confidence, learn teamwork skills, recognize the abilities of those different from them, and improve their physical health. The general public gets to see that athletes do not have to be normally abled people—people of all abilities can participate and compete if they want to.

Diversity in Sports

Natalia Partyka:
Olympic Inspiration

Partyka is one of the few athletes to participate in both the Olympics and the Paralympics.

Some athletes with disabilities participate in the Paralympics or Special Olympics. A few participate in the Olympics, alongside nondisabled athletes. And even fewer do both. Polish table tennis player Natalia Partyka is one of the few who has done both.

Partyka was born in 1989 without her right forearm and hand, but that did not stop her from taking up table tennis when she was seven years old. At age ten, she won an international table tennis medal at the disabled World Championships. The next year, she competed in the 2000 Paralympics held in Sydney, Australia, becoming the world's youngest person to compete in the Paralympics.

Paralympian and Olympian

At the next Paralympics in 2004, Partyka won a gold medal in the singles tournament and a silver medal in the team tournament. That same year she won two gold medals against nondisabled athletes at the International Table Tennis Federation (ITTF) European Championships for Cadets. Partyka continued her winning streak with multiple gold and silver medals in 2006 at the European

Diverse Abilities in Sports

Paralympic Championships, the International Paralympic Committee's Table Tennis World Championships for the Disabled, and the ITTF European Junior Championship. In 2007, she picked up three more gold and a bronze medal at various events.

In 2008, she made the jump to the Olympics, competing at the Summer Olympics and the Summer Paralympics that same year. She was one of only two athletes to do so, along with Natalie du Toit, the South African swimmer. Partyka did the same in 2012, competing at both the Summer Olympics and Summer Paralympics. In both 2008 and 2012, she won gold at the Paralympics. She did not place at the 2008 Olympics but ranked in the top thirty-two at the 2012 Summer Games.

You Can Achieve More than You Think

Partyka does not think much of her disability. She says she gets tired of being asked about it. But she admits that if it inspires someone, then it is worth talking about. She told NBC Sports, "Maybe someone will see me and realize that their own disability is not the end of the world. Maybe someone will look at me and think they can achieve something bigger than they thought. Maybe sometimes you have to work a little bit harder if you really want to do something. If I am an inspiration, I can't complain." Clearly, Partyka has proved that she can work hard for what she wants.

DIFFERENT EVENTS
The International Paralympic Committee (IPC) has broken down impairments into categories of eligibility to ensure the competition is fair. These are impaired muscle power, impaired passive range of movement, limb deficiency, leg length difference, short stature, hypertonia (also known as spasticity—common in conditions such as cerebral palsy), ataxia (lack of muscle coordination), athetosis (another condition that goes accompanies cerebral palsy), vision impairment, and intellectual impairment.

Diversity in Sports

Diversity and Sports: A Winning Combination

Sports is a great place to encourage diversity because everyone can play and work together toward a common goal. Not everyone will be a professional-level athlete, but anyone can play in some way and contribute to a feeling of cooperation and teamwork.

In sports, the focus is on the game and often on winning, not on what makes people different. A good player is a good player, regardless of the many other aspects of who they are. The field, the rink, the court, and the pool are all good places to set aside differences and embrace what is common—a love of sport.

Whether the diversity is based on race, gender, socioeconomic status, culture, or ability, it is beneficial to a team or a group of athletes because everyone brings something different to the table. Different skills, different strategies, different approaches—they can all result in better play. As an example, think of a soccer team. If everyone on a team was a goalkeeper, no doubt the team would have very few goals scored against them. They would be experts at protecting the goal. But soccer is much more than that. Not only does a team have to protect the goal, but it also has to effectively move the ball down the field and score goals on the opposing team.

Diversity can help build better teams, as people from different backgrounds and with different strengths work together.

Diverse Abilities in Sports

A soccer team is best if it has a strong goalkeeper, effective defensive players, and good offensive players. In other words, a soccer team is best if it has diversity—much like every sports team is best if it embraces its players' diversity.

Diversity in sports also brings benefit to spectators and fans. When they see people of different backgrounds, genders, and abilities working together on a team, it promotes a feeling of inclusion that can carry over to the rest of life. If people of different cultures can play together, for example, then why not study together, work together, and live together?

As the United States continues to move further toward being a truly inclusive, accepting society, maybe one of the first places to look at is sports. Sports is, after all, a place where people can come together and have fun.

CRITICAL THINKING QUESTION: What ways can you think of to increase diversity in sports, whether that is in race, gender, socioeconomic background, culture, or ability? How can the United States continue to move forward to a more inclusive model of sports?

43

Timeline

1882: First athletic games for women are held at the YWCA in Boston.

1900: The Olympics begin allowing female athletes to compete.

1908: Jack Johnson, the son of slaves, becomes heavyweight champion after defeating Tommy Burns.

1936: Jesse Owens, a black sprinter from Alabama, earns four Olympic gold medals and breaks three records.

1936: First women's professional basketball team formed.

1943: All-American Girls Softball League formed.

1945: Jackie Robinson becomes the first black player to sign a contract to play for an MLB team.

1948: First Paralympic Games are held.

1949: George Taliaferro becomes the first black man drafted by an NFL team.

1950: Althea Gibson becomes the first black player to compete at the US Nationals in tennis.

1950: Earl Lloyd becomes the first black man to play in the NBA.

1960: Wilma Rudolph becomes the first black woman to win three gold medals in track and field at a single Olympic Games.

1961: Ernie Davis becomes the first black football player to win the Heisman Trophy.

1968: First Special Olympics Summer Games held.

1973: Billie Jean King wins a landmark tennis match against Bobby Riggs, named the Battle of the Sexes.

1974: Black baseball player Hank Aaron breaks the home run record previously set by Babe Ruth.

1975:	Bob Hall becomes the first person to participate in the Boston Marathon in a wheelchair.
1975:	First women's wheelchair basketball tournament is held.
1980:	Sled skiers compete for the first time.
1985:	USWNST plays its first match.
1987:	First annual National Girls and Women in Sports Day held to recognize the accomplishments of female athletes and their struggle for equality in sports.
1988:	Figure skater Debi Thomas becomes the first black woman to medal in figure skating at the Olympics.
1992:	MLB lifts ban on signing women to contracts.
1992:	Manon Rhéaume becomes the first woman to play in an NHL game.
1996:	Women's soccer and women's softball become recognized as Olympic sports. The USWNST wins its first Olympic gold medal.
1997:	The WNBA is established.
1997:	Tiger Woods becomes the youngest golfer to win the Masters—a mere seven years after the Augusta National Golf Club began allowing black people to join the club.
2005:	Danica Patrick becomes the first woman to lead the Indianapolis 500. In 2008, she becomes the first woman to win an IndyCar Series.
2012:	For the first time in history, women outnumber men on the United States Olympic team.
2012:	Gabrielle (Gabby) Douglas becomes the first black gymnast to win the individual all-around gymnastics event at the Olympics.
2016:	Simone Manuel becomes the first black swimmer to win an individual gold Olympic medal.
2016:	For the first time in Olympic history, the US Winter Olympics team features two openly gay men. It also includes twelve Asian-Americans and eleven black team members.

Glossary

civil rights movement A movement for social justice that took place from roughly 1954 to 1968, and involved black people working to gain equal rights to the white people of the United States.

coed An abbreviation for coeducational, which refers to an activity that involves both genders.

dinghy A small inflatable rubber boat.

endorsements Giving public support to products.

ethnicity Belonging to a social group that has a common national or cultural tradition.

FIFA Acronym for Fédération International de Football Association: the governing body of soccer (or football, as it is called in countries other than the United States).

inclusion The act of including different groups of people within a larger group or structure.

indigenous Native peoples of a region.

IndyCar Series A series of popular car races featuring superspeedways, road courses, and temporary street circuits.

intellectual disabilities A disability that affects a person's intelligence or cognitive ability.

Latinx A gender-inclusive form of the word "Latino," often used by Latinos who are genderqueer.

lobotomy A surgical procedure in which an incision is made in the prefrontal lobe of the brain.

polio Short for poliomyelitis: an infectious disease that can cause muscle weakness.

posthumously After death.

Scandinavian Referring to a European region consisting mainly of Norway, Sweden, and Denmark.

Simpson's Diversity Index A measure of diversity that takes into account the number of ethnicities and the abundance of each.

socioeconomic The interaction of social and economic factors.

solidarity Unity or agreement, especially among people with a common interest.

stereotypes Widely held, often simplified beliefs about a particular type of person or thing.

television analyst Someone who analyzes a sports game so that people watching it on television can understand more about the game.

working class People who are employed in manual or industrial jobs, working for hourly wages.

For Further Reading

Books

Edwards, Sue Bradford. *Women in Sports*. Minneapolis, MN: Essential Library, 2016.

Ignotofsky, Rachel. *Women in Sports: 50 Fearless Athletes Who Played to Win*. San Francisco, CA: Ten Speed Press, 2017.

Robinson, Sharon. *Promises to Keep: How Jackie Robinson Changed America*. Scholastic, 2016.

Schaap, Jeremy. *Triumph: The Untold Story of Jesse Owens and Hitler's Olympics*. New York, NY: Mariner Books, 2008.

Websites

Ducksters
www.ducksters.com/sports.php
Ducksters has a lot of useful sporting information, strategies, and more.

Exploratorium
www.exploratorium.edu/explore/sport-science
This website has information about the science behind sports.

Jr. NBA
https://jr.nba.com
The site contains links to all sorts of information about basketball.

Sports Illustrated Kids
www.sikids.com
Sports news, games, and analyses for young sports fans.

Publisher's note to educators and parents: Our editors have carefully reviewed these websites to ensure that they are suitable for students. Many websites change frequently, however, and we cannot guarantee that a site's future contents will continue to meet our high standards of quality and educational value. Be advised that students should be closely supervised whenever they access the Internet.

Index

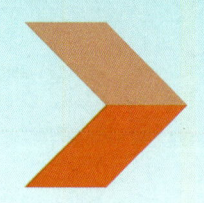

Australian Football League (AFL) 30

baseball 10, 14–15, 16, 17, 20, 24
   All-American Girls Professional Baseball League 16
   Major League Baseball (MLB) 10, 14–15, 16, 17
   Betts, Mookie 10
   Boston Red Sox 10
   Brooklyn Dodgers 14, 15
   Negro Leagues 14, 15
   Robinson, Jackie 14–15
basketball 8–9, 10, 11, 16, 17, 18, 20, 25, 26–27
   Catchings, Tamika 17, 18
   Indiana Fever 17
   National Basketball Association (NBA) 8, 9, 11, 16, 17, 18, 26, 27
   Boston Celtics 17
   Charlotte Hornets 8
   Cuban, Mark 17
   Curry, Dell 8
   Curry, Seth 8
   Curry, Steph 8–9, 26
   Dallas Mavericks 17
   Garnett, Kevin 17
   Golden State Warriors 8
   Griner, Brittney 17
   James, LeBron 26–27
   Women's National Basketball Association (WNBA) 16, 17, 18

common goals 12, 30, 42
culture 4, 5, 6, 22, 28–29, 30, 31, 42, 43

disabilities, athletes with 35–37, 40–41
   du Toit, Natalie 37, 41
   Eyser, George 35
   Fairhall, Neroli 36
   Fantato, Paola 37
   Float, Jeff 36
   Halassy, Olivier 35
   Hartel, Lis 35

Hyun, Im Dong 36
Parkin, Terence 36
Partyka, Natalia 40–41
Újlaky-Rejtő, Ildikó 36
Runyan, Marla 37
Takacs, Karoly 35
diversity
   abilities 34–41
   cultural 28–33
   economic and social 22–27
   gender 16–21, 34
   importance of 5–7, 23, 24, 29, 31, 39, 42–43
   mathematical models of 11, 13
   participation, effect on 23
   pool of players 6, 31
   racial 10–15
   setting an example 6–7, 43
   soccer, in 12–13, 42–43

ethnic background 4, 5, 6, 7, 10, 11, 14, 22, 28, 29
   Asian 10, 11
   black 10, 11, 14, 28
   Latinx 10, 11, 14, 29
   Native American 28, 29
   white 10, 11, 22, 29

figure skating 10, 20
football 6, 10, 25, 27

gender in sports 4, 16–21, 42

integration, sports 17–19, 34–35, 40–41
   benefits of 19, 34
   disability 34–35, 40–41
   gender 17–19
   problems with 18, 34

Mandela, Nelson 29

National Hockey League (NHL) 22, 23

Olympic Games 4, 20, 21, 31, 32–33, 35, 36, 37, 38, 39, 40–41

Paralympic Games 4, 36, 37, 38–39, 40–41
perspectives, unique 5, 31, 42

rags-to-riches stories 24, 26–27
Refugee Olympic Team 32–33
   Anis, Rami 33
   Biel, Yiech 33
   Chiengjiek, James 33
   Kinde, Yonas 33
   Lohalith, Anjelina 33
   Lokonyen, Rose 33
   Lokoro, Paulo 33
   Mabika, Yolande 33
   Mardini, Yusra 32
   Misenga, Popole 33
religious background 6, 9

segregation, sports 4, 16, 34, 39
   by disability 4, 34, 39
   by gender 4, 16, 34
Simpson's Diversity Index 11
soccer 10–11, 12–13, 20–21, 23, 30, 31, 42–43
   Chastain, Brandi 20
   European 12–13
   Hamm, Mia 20
   Major League Soccer (MLS) 10–11, 12, 23
   Solo, Hope 20
   US Women's National Soccer Team (USWNT) 21
   Wambach, Abby 20–21
   Women's World Cup 21
   World Cup 20, 31
socioeconomic background 4, 5, 6, 7, 15, 42, 43
Special Olympics 4, 37, 38–39, 40
   Kennedy, Rosemary 38–39
   Shriver, Eunice Kennedy 38–39
stereotypes 10, 11

table tennis 40–41
teamwork 5, 19, 23, 30, 34, 39, 42

youth sports 30